8th Grade   2007

D0947316

Andrew,
    There's lots of great advice
in here, and it all comes from
the bible!
              Merry Christmas!
                    ~ Mrs. Barons

Life's Little Instructions
from the
BIBLE

H. JACKSON BROWN, JR. AND **ROSEMARY C. BROWN**

Testament Books
New York

This 2005 edition is published by Testament Books, an imprint of Random House Value Publishing, a division of Random House, Inc., New York, by arrangement with Thomas Nelson, Inc., P.O. Box 141000, Nashville, Tennessee 37214-1000.

Random House
New York • Toronto • London • Sydney • Auckland
www.randomhouse.com

Design by Gore Studio

Printed and bound in Singapore

A catalog record for this title is available from the Library of Congress.

ISBN 0-517-22396-1

10 9 8 7 6 5 4 3 2

INTRODUCTION

IT NOW SEEMS INEVITABLE that my words of encouragement and fatherly advice that became the *Life's Little Instruction Book* series would someday inspire a book that my wife, Rosemary, and I would work on together.

As I continued to write books that offered what I knew about living wisely and well, Rosemary was busy studying and writing about life's *original* instruction book, the Bible.

For more than thirty years she has greeted almost every new day in reverent Bible study and prayer. I don't know anyone who loves the Scriptures more or who has read them more devotedly.

Her depth of knowledge made our idea of matching Bible verses with my little instructions an easy and inspiring exercise. And in the process we discovered something unexpected: when you read the fatherly, homespun advice alongside the correlating biblical truths, the former somehow becomes more personal and profound. But we shouldn't have been surprised. The Bible transforms mightily everyone and everything it touches!

Compiling this little book has blessed both of our lives. May you find something valuable here too, as you live your faith and love your God.

— *H. Jackson Brown, Jr.*

For our son, Adam

1 ◆ Compliment three people every day.

A word fitly spoken is like apples of gold in settings of silver. *Proverbs 25:11*

2 ◆ Overtip breakfast waitresses.

A generous man will prosper; he who refreshes others will himself be refreshed. *Proverbs 11:25*

3 • Say "thank you" a lot.

In everything give thanks. *1 Thessalonians 5:18*

4 • Never decide to do nothing just because you can only do a little. Do what you can.

For if the willingness is there, the gift is acceptable according to what one has, not according to what he does not have. *2 Corinthians 8:12*

5 ◆ Learn to play a musical instrument.

Then David spoke to the leaders of the Levites to appoint their brethren to be the singers accompanied by instruments of music, stringed instruments, harps, and cymbals. *1 Chronicles 15:16*

6 ◆ Sing in the shower.

But I will sing of Your power; yes, I will sing aloud of Your mercy in the morning; for You have been my defense and refuge in the day of my trouble. *Psalm 59:16*

7 ◆ Choose your life's mate carefully. From this one decision will come ninety percent of all your happiness or misery.

Who can find a virtuous wife? For her worth is far above rubies. The heart of her husband safely trusts her; so he will have no lack of gain. She does him good and not evil all the days of her life. *Proverbs 31:10–12*

8 ✦ Live beneath your means.

In the house of the wise are stores of choice food and oil, but a foolish man devours all he has. *Proverbs 21:20*

9 ✦ Take along a small gift for the host or hostess when you're a dinner guest. A book is a good choice.

A man's gift makes room for him, and brings him before great men. *Proverbs 18:16*

10 ✦ Become the most positive and optimistic person you know.

I can do all things through Christ who strengthens me.
Philippians 4:13

11 ✦ Return all the things you borrow.

The wicked borrows and does not repay, but the righteous shows mercy and gives. *Psalm 37:21*

12 · Teach some kind of class.

And the things that you have heard from me among many witnesses, commit these to faithful men who will be able to teach others also. *2 Timothy 2:2*

13 · Decide to get up thirty minutes earlier. Do this for a year, and you will add seven and one-half days to your waking world.

I rise before the dawning of the morning, and cry for help; I hope in Your word. *Psalm 119:147*

14 ◆ Worry makes for a hard pillow. When something's troubling you, before going to sleep, jot down three things you can do the next day to help solve the problem.

Be anxious for nothing, but in everything by prayer and supplication, with thanksgiving, let your requests be made known to God; and the peace of God, which surpasses all understanding, will guard your hearts and minds through Christ Jesus. *Philippians 4:6–7*

15 · Keep secrets.

A gossip betrays a confidence; so avoid a man who talks too much. *Proverbs 20:19*

16 · Be better prepared than you think you need to be.

He said to them, "But now if you have a purse, take it, and also a bag; and if you don't have a sword, sell your cloak and buy one." *Luke 22:36*

17 • Don't be thin-skinned. Take criticism as well as praise with equal grace.

Now no chastening seems to be joyful for the present, but grievous; nevertheless, afterward it yields the peaceable fruit of righteousness to those who have been trained by it. *Hebrews 12:11*

18 • Keep a tight rein on your temper.

A patient man has great understanding, but a quick-tempered man displays folly. *Proverbs 14:29*

19 ✦ Pray for our leaders.

Therefore I exhort first of all that supplications, prayers, intercessions, and giving of thanks be made for all men, for kings and all who are in authority, that we may lead a quiet and peaceable life in all godliness and reverence. *1 Timothy 2:1–2*

20 ✦ Learn to bake bread.

So Abraham hurried into the tent to Sarah. "Quick," he said, "get three seahs of fine flour and knead it and bake some bread." *Genesis 18:6*

21 · Make the best of bad situations.

And we know that all things work together for good to those who love God, to those who are the called according to His purpose. *Romans 8:28*

22 · Live so that when your children think of fairness, caring, and integrity, they think of you.

Imitate me, just as I also imitate Christ.
1 Corinthians 11:1

23 ◆ Admit your mistakes.

He who covers his sins will not prosper, but whoever confesses and forsakes them will have mercy.
Proverbs 28:13

24 ◆ Judge your success by the degree that you're enjoying peace, health, and love.

Flee also youthful lusts; but pursue righteousness, faith, love, peace with those who call on the Lord out of a pure heart. *2 Timothy 2:22*

25 · Avoid sarcastic remarks.

But if you bite and devour one another, beware lest you be consumed by one another! *Galatians 5:15*

26 · Choose a charity in your community and support it generously with your time and money.

So let each one give as he purposes in his heart, not grudgingly or of necessity; for God loves a cheerful giver. *2 Corinthians 9:7*

27 ◆ Don't admire people for their wealth but for the creative and generous ways they put it to use.

Command those who are rich in this present age not to be haughty, nor to trust in uncertain riches but in the living God, who gives us richly all things to enjoy. Let them do good, that they be rich in good works, ready to give, willing to share. *1 Timothy 6:17*

28 ⋅ Don't ever let anyone see you tipsy.

And do not be drunk with wine, in which is dissipation; but be filled with the Spirit. *Ephesians 5:18*

29 ⋅ Exercise caution the first day you buy a chain saw. You'll be tempted to cut down everything in the neighborhood.

Wail, O cypress, for the cedar has fallen, because the mighty trees are ruined. Wail, O oaks of Bashan, for the thick forest has come down. *Zechariah 11:2*

30 ✦ Stay humble.

The fear of the Lord is the instruction of wisdom, and before honor is humility. *Proverbs 15:33*

31 ✦ Let your children hear you say things to your wife that lets them know how much you love and treasure her.

Her children arise and call her blessed; her husband also, and he praises her: "Many women do noble things, but you surpass them all." *Proverbs 31:28–29*

32 · Don't forget, a person's greatest emotional need is to feel appreciated.

I thank my God upon every remembrance of you.
Philippians 1:3

33 · Be quick to take advantage of an advantage.

Be wise in the way you act toward outsiders; make the most of every opportunity. *Colossians 4:5*

34 ⋆ Give yourself a year and read the Bible cover to cover.

Your word is a lamp to my feet and a light to my path.
Psalm 119:105

35 ⋆ Once a year, go someplace you've never been before.

Now the Lord had said to Abram: "Get out of your country, from your family and from your father's house, to a land that I will show you." *Genesis 12:1*

36 ✦ Show respect for all living things.

And God made the beast of the earth according to its kind, cattle according to its kind, and everything that creeps on the earth according to its kind. And God saw that it was good. *Genesis 1:25*

37 ✦ Don't buy cheap tools. Craftsman tools from Sears are among the best.

Let him not deceive himself by trusting what is worthless, for he will get nothing in return. *Job 15:31*

38 · Acknowledge every gift, no matter how small.

"She has done what she could. She has before-hand to anoint My body for burial. Assuredly, I say to you, wherever this gospel is preached in the whole world, what this woman has done will also be told as a memorial to her." *Mark 14:8*

39 · When a friend is in need, help him without his having to ask.

Share with God's people who are in need. Practice hospitality. *Romans 12:13*

40 · Accept the fact that regardless of how many times you are right, you will sometimes be wrong.

For we all stumble in many things. *James 3:2*

41 · Ask for a raise when you feel you've earned it.

The laborer is worthy of his wages.   *1 Timothy 5:18*

42 · Measure people by the size of their hearts, not the size of their bank accounts.

"The Lord does not see as man sees; for man looks at the outward appearance, but the Lord looks at the heart."   *1 Samuel 16:7*

43 · Look for the opportunity that's hidden in every adversity.

But as for you, you meant evil against me; but God meant it for good, in order to bring it about as it is this day, to save many people alive. *Genesis 50:20*

44 · Do battle against prejudice and discrimination wherever you find it.

My brothers, as believers in our glorious Lord Jesus Christ, don't show favoritism. *James 2:1*

45 · Never take action when you're angry.

An angry man stirs up strife, and a furious man abounds in transgression. *Proverbs 29:22*

46 · When someone lets you down, don't give up on them.

Then Peter came to Him and said, "Lord, how often shall my brother sin against me, and I forgive him? Up to seven times?" Jesus said to him, "I do not say to you, up to seven times, but up to seventy times seven." *Matthew 18:21–22*

47 ✦ Never give up on what you really want to do. The person with big dreams is more powerful than one with all the facts.

Then they . . . said: "We went to the land where you sent us. It truly flows with milk and honey, and this is its fruit. Nevertheless the people who dwell in the land are strong; the cities are fortified and very large. . . ." Then Caleb . . . said, "Let us go up at once and take possession, for we are well able to overcome it."

Numbers 13:27–30

48 · Surprise a new neighbor with one of your favorite homemade dishes—and include the recipe.

For all the law is fulfilled in one word, even in this: "You shall love your neighbor as yourself." *Galatians 5:14*

49 · Never use profanity.

But now you yourselves are to put off all these: anger, wrath, malice, blasphemy, filthy language out of your mouth. *Colossians 3:8*

50 ✦ Don't watch violent television shows, and don't buy the products that sponsor them.

The Lord tests the righteous, but the wicked and the one who loves violence His soul hates. *Psalm 11:5*

51 ✦ Take responsibility for every area of your life. Stop blaming others.

Then the man said, "The woman whom You gave to be with me, she gave me of the tree, and I ate." *Genesis 3:12*

52 ✦ Never deprive someone of hope. It might be all they have.

Hope deferred makes the heart sick, but when the desire comes, it is a tree of life. *Proverbs 13:12*

53 ✦ Choose work that is in harmony with your values.

Do not be yoked together with unbelievers. For what do righteousness and wickedness have in common? Or what fellowship can light have with darkness? *2 Corinthians 6:14*

54 ◆ Remember that almost everything looks better after a good night's sleep.

I will both lie down in peace, and sleep; for You alone, O Lord, make me dwell in safety. *Psalm 4:8*

55 ◆ Commit yourself to constant self-improvement.

But grow in the grace and knowledge of our Lord and Savior Jesus Christ. To Him be the glory both now and forever. Amen. *2 Peter 3:18*

56 ✦ Observe the speed limit.

Therefore whoever resists the authority resists the ordinance of God, and those who resist will bring judgment on themselves. *Romans 13:2*

57 ✦ Give your best to your employer. It's one of the best investments you can make.

Whatever Saul sent him to do, David did it so successfully that Saul gave him a high rank in the army. *1 Samuel 18:5*

58 · Live your life so that your epitaph could read, "No regrets."

I have fought the good fight, I have finished the race, I have kept the faith. Finally, there is laid up for me the crown of righteousness, which the Lord, the righteous Judge, will give to me on that Day, and not to me only but also to all who have loved His appearing.

2 Timothy 4:7–8

59 ✦ Know when to keep silent. Know when to speak up.

To everything there is a season, a time for every purpose under heaven: . . . a time to keep silence, and a time to speak. *Ecclesiastes 3:1, 7*

60 ✦ Keep your promises.

If a man vows a vow to the Lord, or swears an oath to bind himself by some agreement, he shall not break his word; he shall do according to all that proceeds out of his mouth. *Numbers 30:2*

61 • Spend your life lifting people up, not putting people down.

Your love has given me great joy and encouragement, because you, brother, have refreshed the hearts of the saints. *Philemon 7*

62 • Tell your wife often how terrific she looks.

Behold, you are fair, my love! Behold, you are fair! *Song of Solomon 1:15*

63 • Visit friends and relatives when they are in the hospital. You only need to stay a few minutes.

I was naked and you clothed Me; I was sick and you visited Me; I was in prison and you came to Me.
Matthew 25:36

64 • Be forgiving of yourself and others.

For if you forgive men their trespasses, your heavenly Father will also forgive you. *Matthew 6:14*

65 ◆ Learn to show cheerfulness, even when you don't feel like it.

A happy heart makes the face cheerful, but heartache crushes the spirit. *Proverbs 15:13*

66 ◆ Skip one meal a week and give what you would have spent to a street person.

He who despises his neighbor sins, but blessed is he who is kind to the needy. *Proverbs 14:21*

67 ✦ Every day show your family how much you love them with your words, with your touch, and with your thoughtfulness.

And whatever you do in word or deed, do all in the name of the Lord Jesus, giving thanks to God the Father through Him. *Colossians 3:17*

68 ✦ Don't gossip.

A perverse man stirs up dissension, and a gossip separates close friends. *Proverbs 16:28*

69 ◆ Don't nag.

With such nagging she prodded him day after day until he was tired to death. *Judges 16:16*

70 ◆ Take a few hours every month to deliver Meals on Wheels.

If a brother or sister is naked and destitute of daily food, and one of you says to them, "Depart in peace, be warmed and filled," but you do not give them the things which are needed for the body, what does it profit? *James 2:15–16*

71 ✦ Lie on your back and look at the stars.

The sun has one kind of splendor, the moon another and the stars another; and star differs from star in splendor. *1 Corinthians 15:41*

72 ✦ Don't expect money to bring you happiness.

Take heed and beware of covetousness, for one's life does not consist in the abundance of the things he possesses. *Luke 12:15*

73 ✦ Don't whine.

Do everything without complaining or arguing.
Philippians 2:14

74 ✦ When facing a difficult task, act as though it is impossible to fail. If you're going after Moby Dick, take along the tartar sauce.

But Jesus looked at them and said, "With men it is impossible, but not with God; for with God all things are possible." *Mark 10:27*

75 ◆ Remember that what's right isn't always popular, and what's popular isn't always right.

Bloodthirsty men hate a man of integrity and seek to kill the upright. *Proverbs 29:10*

76 ◆ Keep expectations high.

In the morning, O Lord, You hear my voice; in the morning I lay my requests before You and wait in expectation. *Psalm 5:3*

77 ✦ When you arrive at your job in the morning, let the first thing you say brighten everyone's day.

The wise in heart are called discerning, and pleasant words promote instruction.   *Proverbs 16:21*

78 ✦ Pay attention to the details.

And in the eleventh year, in the month of Bul, which is the eighth month, the house was finished in all its details and according to all its plans. So he was seven years in building it.   *1 Kings 6:38*

79 ✦ Never eat the last cookie.

When you reap the harvest of your land, you shall not wholly reap the corners of your field when you reap, nor shall you gather any gleaning from your harvest. You shall leave them for the poor and for the stranger.

Leviticus 23:22

80 · Be bold and courageous. When you look back on your life, you'll regret the things you didn't do more than the ones you did.

Have I not commanded you? Be strong and of good courage; do not be afraid, nor be dismayed, for the Lord your God is with you wherever you go. *Joshua 1:9*

81 · Be courteous to everyone.

Let your speech always be with grace, seasoned with salt, that you may know how you ought to answer each one. *Colossians 4:6*

82 · Refrain from envy. It's the source of much unhappiness.

A sound heart is life to the body, but envy is rottenness to the bones. *Proverbs 14:30*

83 · Accept pain and disappointment as part of life.

Beloved, do not think it strange concerning the fiery trial which is to try you, as though some strange thing happened to you. *1 Peter 4:12*

84 • Don't waste time grieving over past mistakes. Learn from them and move on.

But one thing I do, forgetting those things which are behind and reaching forward to those things which are ahead, I press toward the goal for the prize of the upward call of God in Christ Jesus. *Philippians 3:13–14*

85 · Don't postpone joy.

Rejoice always.   *1 Thessalonians 5:16*

86 · Remember that silence is sometimes the best answer.

He was oppressed and He was afflicted, yet He opened not His mouth; He was led as a lamb to the slaughter, and as a sheep before its shearers is silent, so He opened not his mouth.   *Isaiah 53:7*

87 ◆ Whenever you hear an ambulance siren, say a prayer for the person inside.

Pray for one another, that you may be healed. The effective, fervent prayer of a righteous man avails much.
James 5:16

88 ◆ Evaluate yourself by your own standards, not someone else's.

Each one should test his own actions. Then he can take pride in himself, without comparing himself to somebody else. *Galatians 6:4*

89 · Keep good company.

Do not be misled: "Bad company corrupts good character." *1 Corinthians 15:33*

90 · Be brave. Even if you're not, pretend to be. No one can tell the difference.

Be strong and of good courage, do not fear nor be afraid of them; for the Lord your God, He is the One who goes with you. He will not leave you nor forsake you. *Deuteronomy 31:6*

91 · Spend some time alone.

Be still, and know that I am God. *Psalm 46:10*

92 · Learn how to handle a handsaw and a hammer.

"And Bezalel and Aholiab, and every gifted artisan in whom the Lord has put wisdom and understanding, to know how to do all manner of work for the service of the sanctuary, shall do according to all that the Lord has commanded." *Exodus 36:1*

93 ✦ Be loyal.

But Ruth said: "Entreat me not to leave you, or to turn back from following after you; for wherever you go, I will go; and wherever you lodge, I will lodge; your people shall be my people, and your God, my God. Where you die, I will die, and there will I be buried. The Lord do so to me, and more also, if anything but death parts you and me." *Ruth 1:16–17*

94 · Be enthusiastic about the success of others.

And if one member suffers, all the members suffer with it; or if one member is honored, all the members rejoice with it. *1 Corinthians 12:26*

95 · When tempted to criticize your parents, spouse, or children, bite your tongue.

Whoever curses his father or his mother, his lamp will be put out in deep darkness. *Proverbs 20:20*

96 · Never compromise your integrity.

The integrity of the upright will guide them, but the perversity of the unfaithful will destroy them.
Proverbs 11:3

97 · Do more than is expected.

And whoever compels you to go one mile, go with him two. *Matthew 5:41*

98 ✦ Never go to bed with dishes in the sink.

She watches over the ways of her household, and does not eat the bread of idleness.   *Proverbs 31:27*

99 ✦ Just to see how it feels, for the next twenty-four hours refrain from criticizing anybody or anything.

But why do you judge your brother? Or why do you show contempt for your brother? For we shall all stand before the judgment seat of Christ.   *Romans 14:10*

100 ✦ Never "borrow" so much as a pencil from your workplace.

You shall not steal. *Exodus 20:15*

101 ✦ Do a good job because you want to, not because you have to. This puts you in charge instead of your boss.

Do you see a man who excels in his work? He will stand before kings; he will not stand before unknown men. *Proverbs 22:29*

102 ✦ Don't be afraid to say, "I need help."

Let us therefore come boldly to the throne of grace, that we may obtain mercy and find grace to help in time of need. *Hebrews 4:16*

103 ✦ Don't be afraid to say, "I'm sorry."

David said to the Lord, "I have sinned greatly in what I have done; but now, I pray, O Lord, take away the iniquity of Your servant, for I have done very foolishly." *2 Samuel 24:10*

104 ◆ What you must do, do cheerfully.

All the days of the afflicted are evil, but he who is of a merry heart has a continual feast. *Proverbs 15:15*

105 ◆ Mind your own business.

Aspire to lead a quiet life, to mind your own business, and to work with your own hands, as we commanded you, that you may walk properly toward those who are outside, and that you may lack nothing.
1 Thessalonians 4:11–12

106 • Don't be rushed into making an important decision. People will understand if you say, "I'd like a little more time to think it over. Can I get back to you tomorrow?"

Do you see a man hasty in his words? There is more hope for a fool than for him.   *Proverbs 29:20*

107 ◆ Give thanks before every meal.

And Jesus took the loaves, and when He had given thanks He distributed them to the disciples, and the disciples to those sitting down; and likewise of the fish, as much as they wanted. *John 6:11*

108 ◆ Learn to show enthusiasm, even when you don't feel like it.

Never be lacking in zeal, but keep your spiritual fervor, serving the Lord. *Romans 12:11*

109 ✦ Don't expect others to listen to your advice and ignore your example.

In everything set them an example by doing what is good. *Titus 2:7*

110 ✦ Go the distance. When you accept a task, finish it.

Now finish the work, so that your eager willingness to do it may be matched by your completion of it, according to your means. *2 Corinthians 8:11*

111 ◆ Be a student in some kind of class.

Listen to advice and accept instruction, and in the end you will be wise. *Proverbs 19:20*

112 ◆ Commit yourself to quality.

Now if anyone builds on this foundatic
silver, precious stones, wood, hay, str?
will become clear; for the Day wil¹
it will be revealed by fire; and ʈ¹
work, of what sort it is. *1 Cor.*

113 · Never underestimate the power of words to heal and reconcile relationships.

A wholesome tongue is a tree of life, but perverseness in it breaks the spirit. *Proverbs 15:4*

114 · Take care of your reputation. It's your most valuable asset.

A good name is more desirable than great riches; to be esteemed is better than silver or gold. *Proverbs 22:1*

115 ◆ Pray. There is immeasurable power in it.

Pray without ceasing.   *1 Thessalonians 5:17*

116 ◆ Life is short. Eat more pancakes and fewer rice cakes.

So I commend the enjoyment of life, because nothing is better for a man under the sun than to eat and drink and be glad. Then joy will accompany him in his work all the days of the life God has given him under the sun. *Ecclesiastes 8:15*

117 ◆ Pay your bills on time.

Render therefore to all their due: taxes to whom taxes are due, customs to whom customs, fear to whom fear, honor to whom honor. *Romans 13:7*

118 ◆ Learn to make great chili.

Now Jacob cooked a stew; and Esau came in from the field, and he was weary. And Esau said to Jacob, "Please feed me with that same red stew, for I am weary."
Genesis 25:29–30

119 ✦ A racehorse that consistently runs just a second faster than another horse is worth millions of dollars more. Be willing to give that extra effort that separates the winner from the one in second place.

Do you not know that those who run in a race all run, but one receives the prize? Run in such a way that you may obtain it. *1 Corinthians 9:24*

120 ✦ Donate two pints of blood every year.

The life of all flesh is its blood. *Leviticus 17:14*

121 ✦ Make allowances for your friends' imperfections as readily as you do for your own.

And why do you look at the speck in your brother's eye, but do not perceive the plank in your own eye? *Luke 6:41*

122 · Don't miss the magic of the moment by focusing on what's to come.

Therefore do not worry about tomorrow, for tomorrow will worry about its own things.   *Matthew 6:34*

123 · Never watch a movie or video with your children that involves activities and language that you don't want them to imitate.

Turn away my eyes from looking at worthless things, and revive me in Your way.   *Psalm 119:37*

124 ◆ Be the first to forgive.

A man's wisdom gives him patience; it is to his glory to overlook an offense. *Proverbs 19:11*

125 ◆ Turn enemies into friends by doing something nice for them.

But love your enemies, do good, and lend, hoping for nothing in return; and your reward will be great, and you will be sons of the Highest. *Luke 6:35*

126 ◆ Hold yourself to the highest standards.

Not that I have already attained, or am already perfected; but I press on, that I may lay hold of that for which Christ Jesus has also laid hold of me.

Philippians 3:12

127 ◆ Remember that a person who is foolish with money is foolish in other ways too.

Of what use is money in the hand of a fool, since he has no desire to get wisdom? *Proverbs 17:16*

128 · Don't carry a grudge.

You shall not take vengeance, nor bear any grudge . . . ,
but you shall love your neighbor as yourself.
Leviticus 19:18

129 · Be an original. If that means being a little eccentric, so be it.

I will praise You, for I am fearfully and wonderfully
made; marvelous are Your works, and that my soul
knows very well. *Psalm 139:14*

130 ✦ Be as friendly to the janitor as you are to the chairman of the board.

For if there should come into your assembly a man with gold rings, in fine apparel, and there should also come in a poor man in filthy clothes, and you pay attention to the one wearing the fine clothes and say to him, "You sit here in a good place," and say to the poor man, "You stand there," or, "Sit here at my footstool," have you not shown partiality among yourselves, and become judges with evil thoughts? *James 2:2–4*

131 • Do the right thing, regardless of what others think.

And you shall do what is right and good in the sight of the Lord, that it may be well with you, and that you may go in and possess the good land of which the Lord swore to your fathers. *Deuteronomy 6:18*

132 • Avoid like the plague any lawsuit.

They make many promises, take false oaths and make agreements; therefore lawsuits spring up like poisonous weeds in a plowed field. *Hosea 10:4*

133 ✦ Remember that it is easier to avoid temptations than to resist them.

In the paths of the wicked lie thorns and snares, but he who guards his soul stays far from them. *Proverbs 22:5*

134 ✦ Always put something in the collection plate.

But this I say: He who sows sparingly will also reap sparingly, and he who sows bountifully will also reap bountifully. *2 Corinthians 9:6*

135 ◆ Watch your attitude. It's the first thing people notice about you.

You were taught, with regard to your former way of life, to put off your old self, which is being corrupted by its deceitful desires; to be made new in the attitude of your minds; and to put on the new self, created to be like God in true righteousness and holiness.

Ephesians 4:22–24

136 ✦ Plant flowers every spring.

The flowers appear on the earth; the time of singing has come. *Song of Solomon 2:12*

137 ✦ When you find someone doing small things well, put him or her in charge of bigger things.

His lord said to him, "Well done, good and faithful servant; you were faithful over a few things, I will make you ruler over many things. Enter into the joy of your lord." *Matthew 25:21*

138 ✦ Become your children's best teacher and coach.

And you, fathers, do not provoke your children to wrath, but bring them up in the training and admonition of the Lord. *Ephesians 6:4*

139 ✦ When asked to pray in public, be quick about it.

And when you pray, do not keep on babbling like pagans, for they think they will be heard because of their many words. *Matthew 6:7*

140 ◆ Be the kind of person who brightens a room just by entering it.

Let your light so shine before men, that they may see your good works and glorify your Father in heaven.
Matthew 5:16

141 • Volunteer to work a few hours each month in a soup kitchen.

For I was hungry and you gave Me food; I was thirsty and you gave Me drink; I was a stranger and you took Me in. *Matthew 25:35*

142 • Champion your wife. Be her best friend and biggest fan.

Therefore a man shall leave his father and mother and be joined to his wife, and they shall become one flesh. *Genesis 2:24*

143 • Don't accept unacceptable behavior.

Why do you make me look at injustice? Why do you tolerate wrong? Destruction and violence are before me; there is strife, and conflict abounds. Therefore the law is paralyzed, and justice never prevails. The wicked hem in the righteous, so that justice is perverted. *Habakkuk 1:3–4*

144 • Swing for the fence.

Be diligent in these matters; give yourself wholly to them, so that everyone may see your progress.
1 Timothy 4:15

145 · Don't be afraid to say, "I made a mistake."

I will arise and go to my father, and will say to him, "Father, I have sinned against heaven and before you, and I am no longer worthy to be called your son. Make me like one of your hired servants." And he arose and came to his father. But when he was still a great way off, his father saw him and had compassion, and ran and fell on his neck and kissed him. *Luke 15:18–20*

146 ⬧ Write "thank you" notes promptly.

I . . . do not cease to give thanks for you, making mention of you in my prayers. *Ephesians 1:16*

147 ⬧ At the end of your days, be leaning forward—not falling backward.

And now, here I am this day, eighty-five years old. As yet I am as strong this day as I was on the day that Moses sent me; just as my strength was then, so now is my strength for war, both for going out and for coming in. *Joshua 14:10–11*

148 ✦ Be wary of the man who is "all hat and no cattle."

Stop judging by mere appearances, and make a right judgment. *John 7:24*

149 ✦ Keep impeccable tax records.

And He said to them, "Render therefore to Caesar the things that are Caesar's, and to God the things that are God's." *Matthew 22:21*

150 ✦ Never push away a child.

But Jesus said, "Let the little children come to Me, and do not forbid them; for of such is the kingdom of heaven." *Matthew 19:14*

151 ✦ Smile a lot. It costs nothing and is beyond price.

When I smiled at them, they scarcely believed it; the light of my face was precious to them. *Job 29:24*

152 · When traveling the backroads, stop whenever you see a sign that reads "Honey for Sale."

My son, eat honey because it is good, and the honeycomb which is sweet to your taste. *Proverbs 24:13*

153 · Never forget that contentment is the greatest wealth.

But godliness with contentment is great gain.
1 Timothy 6:6

154 ✦ Your mind can only hold one thought at a time. Make it a positive and constructive one.

Finally, brethren, whatever things are true, whatever things are noble, whatever things are just, whatever things are pure, whatever things are lovely, whatever things are of good report, if there is any virtue and if there is anything praiseworthy—meditate on these things. *Philippians 4:8*

155 ⬩ Never waste an opportunity to tell good employees how much they mean to the company.

"Well done, good servant; because you were faithful in a very little, have authority over ten cities."
Luke 19:17

156 ⬩ Be truthful in all your dealings.

An honest answer is like a kiss on the lips.
Proverbs 24:26

157 ◆ Keep candles and matches in the kitchen and bedroom in case of power failure.

Those who were foolish took their lamps and took no oil with them, but the wise took oil in their vessels with their lamps. *Matthew 25:3–4*

158 ◆ Always offer guests something to eat or drink when they drop by.

Be hospitable to one another without grumbling. *1 Peter 4:9*

159 ✦ Learn to recognize the inconsequential; then ignore it.

So we fix our eyes not on what is seen, but on what is unseen. For what is seen is temporary, but what is unseen is eternal. *2 Corinthians 4:18*

160 ✦ Remember the old proverb, "Out of debt, out of danger."

Owe no one anything except to love one another, for he who loves another has fulfilled the law. *Romans 13:8*

161 ⋅ Keep your desk and work area neat.

But everything should be done in a fitting and orderly way.   *1 Corinthians 14:40*

162 ⋅ Encourage anyone who is trying to improve mentally, physically, or spiritually.

Let us not give up meeting together, as some are in the habit of doing, but let us encourage one another— and all the more as you see the Day approaching. *Hebrews 10:25*

163 • Never be ashamed of laughter that's too loud or singing that's too joyful.

Then our mouth was filled with laughter, and our tongue with singing. Then they said among the nations, "The Lord has done great things for them." *Psalm 126:2*

164 • When you get really angry, stick your hands in your pockets.

Cease from anger, and forsake wrath; do not fret—it only causes harm. *Psalm 37:8*

165 ✦ Don't mistake kindness for weakness.

Or do you show contempt for the riches of his kindness, tolerance and patience, not realizing that God's kindness leads you toward repentance? *Romans 2:4*

166 ✦ Truth is serious business. When criticizing others, remember that a little goes a long way.

Judge not, and you shall not be judged. Condemn not, and you shall not be condemned. Forgive, and you will be forgiven. *Luke 6:37*

167 ✦ When reading self-help books, include the Bible.

How can a young man keep his way pure? By living according to Your word.   *Psalm 119:9*

168 ✦ Remember that the more you know, the less you fear.

For God has not given us a spirit of fear, but of power and of love and of a sound mind.   *2 Timothy 1:7*

169 ◆ Let some things remain mysterious.

Then [Delilah] said to [Samson], "How can you say, 'I love you,' when you won't confide in me? This is the third time you have made a fool of me and haven't told me the secret of your great strength." . . . So he told her everything. . . . When Delilah saw that he had told her everything, she . . . called a man to shave off the seven braids of his hair, and so began to subdue him. And his strength left him. *Judges 16:15–19*

170 ✦ Never get a tattoo.

You shall not make any cuttings in your flesh for the dead, nor tattoo any marks on you. *Leviticus 19:28*

171 ✦ When you pass a family riding in a big U-Haul truck, give them the "thumbs-up" sign. They need all the encouragement they can get.

Therefore encourage one another and build each other up, just as in fact you are doing. *1 Thessalonians 5:11*

172 • Watch your language.

Whoever guards his mouth and tongue keeps his soul from troubles. *Proverbs 21:23*

173 • Don't work for recognition, but do work worthy of recognition.

We . . . pray for you, . . . that you may walk worthy of the Lord, fully pleasing Him, being fruitful in every good work and increasing in the knowledge of God.
Colossians 1:9–10

174 • Be kinder than necessary.

Blessed are the merciful, for they shall obtain mercy.
Matthew 5:7

175 • Remember that some things are best understood by the heart and not by the mind.

For we walk by faith, not by sight. *2 Corinthians 5:7*

176 • Treat everyone you meet like you want to be treated.

And just as you want men to do to you, you also do to them likewise. *Luke 6:31*

177 • Stay out of nightclubs.

You are all sons of light and sons of the day. We are not of the night nor of darkness. Therefore let us not sleep, as others do, but let us watch and be sober. For those who sleep, sleep at night, and those who get drunk are drunk at night. *1 Thessalonians 5:5–7*

178 · Win without boasting.

Thus says the Lord: "Let not the wise man glory in his wisdom, let not the mighty man glory in his might, nor let the rich man glory in his riches; but let him who glories glory in this, that he understands and knows Me, that I am the Lord, exercising lovingkindness, judgment, and righteousness in the earth. For in these I delight," says the Lord. *Jeremiah 9:23–24*

179 • Love someone who doesn't deserve it.

But when the kindness and the love of God our Savior toward man appeared, not by works of righteousness which we have done, but according to His mercy He saved us. *Titus 3:4–5*

180 • When you mean no, say it in a way that's not ambiguous.

But let your "Yes" be "Yes," and your "No," "No." *Matthew 5:37*

181 ◆ Keep your private thoughts private.

A prudent man keeps his knowledge to himself, but the heart of fools blurts out folly. *Proverbs 12:23*

182 ◆ Never allow anyone to intimidate you.

Then David said to the Philistine, "You come to me with a sword, with a spear, and with a javelin. But I come to you in the name of the Lord of hosts, the God of the armies of Israel, whom you have defied." *1 Samuel 17:45*

183 · Never forget that it takes only one person or one idea to change your life forever.

Therefore, if anyone is in Christ, he is a new creation; old things have passed away; behold, all things have become new. *2 Corinthians 5:17*

184 ✦ Act with courtesy and fairness regardless of how others treat you. Don't let them determine your response.

And if you do good to those who do good to you, what credit is that to you? For even sinners do the same. *Luke 6:33*

185 ✦ Include your parents in your prayers.

Honor your father and your mother, that your days may be long upon the land which the Lord your God is giving you. *Exodus 20:12*

186 ◆ Remember that how you say something is as important as what you say.

A soft answer turns away wrath, but a harsh word stirs up anger. *Proverbs 15:1*

187 ◆ Never hesitate to do what you know is right.

Blessed are they who maintain justice, who constantly do what is right. *Psalm 106:3*

188 ✦ Grind it out. Hanging on just one second longer than your competition makes you the winner.

We want each of you to show this same diligence to the very end, in order to make your hope sure. We do not want you to become lazy, but to imitate those who through faith and patience inherit what has been promised. *Hebrews 6:11–12*

189 ◆ Hire people more for their judgment than for their talents.

My son, preserve sound judgment and discernment, do not let them out of your sight; they will be life for you, an ornament to grace your neck. *Proverbs 3:21–22*

190 ◆ Think twice before burdening a friend with a secret.

Cast your burden on the Lord, and He shall sustain you; He shall never permit the righteous to be moved. *Psalm 55:22*

191 • Forgive quickly.

And whenever you stand praying, if you have anything against anyone, forgive him, that your Father in heaven may also forgive you your trespasses. *Mark 11:25*

192 • Kiss slowly.

Let him kiss me with the kisses of his mouth—for your love is better than wine. *Song of Solomon 1:2*

193 · Remember that the word *discipline* means "to teach."

Whoever loves discipline loves knowledge, but he who hates correction is stupid. *Proverbs 12:1*

194 · Don't let your possessions possess you.

For we brought nothing into this world, and it is certain we can carry nothing out. *1 Timothy 6:7*

195 • Remember the ones who love you.

I thank my God, making mention of you always in my prayers. *Philemon 4*

196 • Don't use time or words carelessly. Neither can be retrieved.

But I say to you that for every idle word men may speak, they will give account of it in the day of judgment. *Matthew 12:36*

197 ✦ Remember that your child's character is like good soup. Both are homemade.

Only be careful, and watch yourselves closely so that you do not forget the things your eyes have seen or let them slip from your heart as long as you live. Teach them to your children and to their children after them.

Deuteronomy 4:9

198 ✦ Never cheat.

Therefore, rid yourselves of all malice and all deceit, hypocrisy, envy, and slander of every kind.   *1 Peter 2:1*

199 ✦ Find a job you love and give it everything you've got.

And in every work that he began in the service of the house of God, in the law and in the commandment, to seek his God, he did it with all his heart. So he prospered. *2 Chronicles 31:21*

200 ✦ Say something positive as early as possible every day.

Anxiety in the heart of man causes depression, but a good word makes it glad. *Proverbs 12:25*

201 · Seek respect rather than popularity.

On the contrary, we speak as men approved by God to be entrusted with the gospel. We are not trying to please men but God, who tests our hearts. *1 Thessalonians 2:4*

202 · Give people a second chance, but not a third.

Warn a divisive person once, and then warn him a second time. After that, have nothing to do with him. *Titus 3:10*

203 ✦ Fly Old Glory on the Fourth of July.

Lift up a banner for the peoples! *Isaiah 62:10*

204 ✦ Remember that the more you judge the people in your life, the more unhappy you'll be.

Therefore you are inexcusable, O man, whoever you are who judge, for in whatever you judge another you condemn yourself; for you who judge practice the same things. *Romans 2:1*

205 · If you are not going to use a discount coupon, leave it on the shelf with the product for someone else to use.

As she got up to glean, Boaz gave orders to his men, "Even if she gathers among the sheaves, don't embarrass her. Rather, pull out some stalks for her from the bundles and leave them for her to pick up, and don't rebuke her." *Ruth 2:15–16*

206 ◆ Do something every day that maintains your good health.

Or do you not know that your body is the temple of the Holy Spirit who is in you, whom you have from God, and you are not your own? *1 Corinthians 6:19*

207 ◆ Remember that what you give will afford you more pleasure than what you get.

It is more blessed to give than to receive. *Acts 20:35*

208 ✦ Don't get too big for your britches.

Now this is what the Lord Almighty says: "Give careful thought to your ways." *Haggai 1:5*

209 ✦ Regardless of the situation, remember that following the Golden Rule is always the best approach.

Therefore, whatever you want men to do to you, do also to them, for this is the Law and the Prophets. *Matthew 7:12*

210 ✦ Remember that a grateful heart is almost always a happy one.

The Lord is my strength and my shield; my heart trusted in Him, and I am helped; therefore my heart greatly rejoices, and with my song I will praise Him.
Psalm 28:7

211 ✦ Never waste an opportunity to tell someone you love them.

As the Father loved Me, I also have loved you; abide in My love.   *John 15:9*

212 ◆ Worry about the consequences of the choices you make before you make them—not afterward.

It is a trap for a man to dedicate something rashly and only later to consider his vows. *Proverbs 20:25*

213 ◆ What you have to do, do wholeheartedly.

Serve wholeheartedly, as if you were serving the Lord, not men. *Ephesians 6:7*

214 ◆ Stay on your toes.

Be sober, be vigilant; because your adversary the devil walks about like a roaring lion, seeking whom he may devour. *1 Peter 5:8*

215 ◆ Be willing to swap a temporary inconvenience for a permanent improvement.

For our light affliction, which is but for a moment, is working for us a far more exceeding and eternal weight of glory. *2 Corinthians 4:17*

216 ⋆ Remember that a lasting marriage is built on commitment, not convenience.

And He answered and said to them, "Have you not read that He who made them at the beginning 'made them male and female,' and said, 'For this reason a man shall leave his father and mother and be joined to his wife, and the two shall become one flesh'? So then, they are no longer two but one flesh. Therefore what God has joined together, let not man separate."

Matthew 19:4–6

217 · Pray not for things, but for wisdom and courage.

I keep asking that the God of our Lord Jesus Christ, the glorious Father, may give you the Spirit of wisdom and revelation, so that you may know Him better.

Ephesians 1:17

218 · Remember that cruel words deeply hurt.

Reckless words pierce like a sword, but the tongue of the wise brings healing. *Proverbs 12:18*

219 · Remember that loving words quickly heal.

Pleasant words are like a honeycomb, sweetness to the soul and health to the bones. *Proverbs 16:24*

220 · When you're the first one up, be quiet about it.

He who blesses his friend with a loud voice, rising early in the morning, it will be counted a curse to him. *Proverbs 27:14*

221 · Never ignore your car's oil warning
light.

A prudent man sees danger and takes refuge, but the
simple keep going and suffer for it. *Proverbs 22:3*

222 · When a guest, never complain about the
food, drink, or accommodations.

Whatever city you enter, and they receive you, eat
such things as are set before you. *Luke 10:8*

223 ✦ Never underestimate the power of love.

Love never fails. *1 Corinthians 13:8*

224 ✦ Never forget the debt you owe to all those who have come before you.

Now, therefore, you are no longer strangers and foreigners, but fellow citizens with the saints and members of the household of God, having been built on the foundation of the apostles and prophets, Jesus Christ Himself being the chief cornerstone. *Ephesians 2:19–20*

225 · When opportunity knocks, invite it to stay for dinner.

Then the Lord appeared to him by the terebinth trees of Mamre, as he was sitting in the tent door in the heat of the day. So he lifted his eyes and looked, and behold, three men were standing by him; and when he saw them, he ran from the tent door to meet them, and bowed himself to the ground, and said, "My Lord, if I have now found favor in Your sight, do not pass on by Your servant. Please let a little water be brought, and wash your feet, and rest yourselves under the tree. And I will bring a morsel of bread, that you may refresh your hearts." *Genesis 18:1–5*

226 ✦ Create and maintain a peaceful home.

Better a dry crust with peace and quiet than a house full of feasting, with strife. *Proverbs 17:1*

227 ✦ Never call anybody stupid, even if you're kidding.

But I say to you that whoever is angry with his brother without a cause shall be in danger of the judgment. . . . But whoever says, "You fool!" shall be in danger of hell fire. *Matthew 5:22*

228 ◆ Never buy an article of clothing thinking it will fit if you lose a couple of pounds.

Do not boast about tomorrow, for you do not know what a day may bring forth. *Proverbs 27:1*

229 ◆ Rebuild a broken relationship.

Now all things are of God, who has reconciled us to Himself through Jesus Christ, and has given us the ministry of reconciliation. *2 Corinthians 5:18*

230 ◆ Watch your finances like a hawk.

Be diligent to know the state of your flocks, and attend to your herds; for riches are not forever, nor does a crown endure to all generations. *Proverbs 27:23–24*

231 ◆ Commit yourself to a mighty purpose.

Speak up for those who cannot speak for themselves, for the rights of all who are destitute. Speak up and judge fairly; defend the rights of the poor and needy. *Proverbs 31:8–9*

232 ◆ Respect your elders.

You shall rise before the gray headed and honor the presence of an old man, and fear your God.
Leviticus 19:32

233 ◆ Never betray a confidence.

A gossip betrays a confidence, but a trustworthy man keeps a secret. *Proverbs 11:13*

234 ◆ Be prudent.

The simple inherit folly, but the prudent are crowned with knowledge. *Proverbs 14:18*

235 ◆ Listen to your favorite music while working on your tax return.

And so it was, whenever the spirit from God was upon Saul, that David would take a harp and play it with his hand. Then Saul would become refreshed and well, and the distressing spirit would depart from him.
1 Samuel 16:23

236 · Never ignore evil.

Hate what is evil; cling to what is good.   *Romans 12:9*

237 · Remember that you can miss a lot of good things in life by having the wrong attitude.

Your attitude should be the same as that of Christ Jesus.   *Philippians 2:5*

238 ✦ Contribute something to each Salvation Army kettle you pass during the holidays.

Now He who supplies seed to the sower and bread for food will also supply and increase your store of seed and will enlarge the harvest of your righteousness. You will be made rich in every way so that you can be generous on every occasion, and through us your generosity will result in thanksgiving to God. *2 Corinthians 9:10–11*

239 · Regarding rental property, remember that an unrented house is better than a bad tenant.

At harvest time he sent a servant to the tenants so they would give him some of the fruit of the vineyard. But the tenants beat him and sent him away empty-handed. *Luke 20:10*

240 · Never resist a generous impulse.

But do not forget to do good and to share, for with such sacrifices God is well pleased. *Hebrews 13:16*

241 · **When someone you know is down and out, mail them a twenty-dollar bill anonymously.**

Give generously to him and do so without a grudging heart; then because of this the Lord your God will bless you in all your work and in everything you put your hand to. *Deuteronomy 15:10*

242 · **Teach by example.**

Be an example to the believers in word, in conduct, in love, in spirit, in faith, in purity. *1 Timothy 4:12*

243 ◆ Remember that ignorance is expensive.

My people are destroyed for lack of knowledge.
Hosea 4:6

244 ◆ Remember that nothing important was ever achieved without someone's taking a chance.

We had previously suffered and been insulted in Philippi, as you know, but with the help of our God we dared to tell you His gospel in spite of strong opposition.
1 Thessalonians 2:2

245 ◆ Stand up for your high principles even if you have to stand alone.

At my first defense no one stood with me, but all forsook me. May it not be charged against them.
2 Timothy 4:16

246 ◆ Remember that a minute of anger denies you sixty seconds of happiness.

For man's anger does not bring about the righteous life that God desires. *James 1:20*

247 · Be faithful.

Marriage should be honored by all, and the marriage bed kept pure, for God will judge the adulterer and all the sexually immoral. *Hebrews 13:4*

248 · Laugh a lot. A good sense of humor cures almost all of life's ills.

A merry heart does good, like medicine, but a broken spirit dries the bones. *Proverbs 17:22*

249 ✦ Eat moderately.

Do not join those who drink too much wine or gorge themselves on meat, for drunkards and gluttons become poor, and drowsiness clothes them in rags.
Proverbs 23:20–21

250 ✦ Don't let a little dispute injure a great friendship.

Make every effort to keep the unity of the Spirit through the bond of peace. *Ephesians 4:3*

251 ✦ Take an hour to cool off before responding to someone who has provoked you. If it involves something really important, take overnight.

Better a patient man than a warrior, a man who controls his temper than one who takes a city.
Proverbs 16:32

252 · Don't gamble.

Ill-gotten treasures are of no value, but righteousness delivers from death. *Proverbs 10:2*

253 · Show gratitude, if not for what you have now, then for all the good things still ahead.

But as it is written: "Eye has not seen, nor ear heard, nor have entered into the heart of man the things which God has prepared for those who love Him." *1 Corinthians 2:9*

254 ✦ Report unethical business practices to your city's Better Business Bureau.

Do not have two differing weights in your bag—one heavy, one light. . . . For the Lord your God detests anyone who does these things, anyone who deals dishonestly. *Deuteronomy 25:13, 16*

255 ✦ Don't spend lots of time with couples who criticize each other.

It is to a man's honor to avoid strife, but every fool is quick to quarrel. *Proverbs 20:3*

256 ✦ Work diligently.

He who has a slack hand becomes poor, but the hand of the diligent makes rich. *Proverbs 10:4*

257 ✦ Bad things happen in bad places, so stay out of bad places.

Watch and pray so that you will not fall into temptation. The spirit is willing, but the body is weak. *Matthew 26:41*

258 • Vote.

When the righteous triumph, there is great elation; but when the wicked rise to power, men go into hiding.
Proverbs 28:12

259 • Donate food for natural disaster victims when you see a display in a store.

He answered and said to them, "He who has two tunics, let him give to him who has none; and he who has food, let him do likewise." *Luke 3:11*

260 ✦ Sing out in church; God isn't a music critic.

Shout joyfully to the Lord, all the earth; break forth in song, rejoice, and sing praises. *Psalm 98:4*

261 ✦ When you make it big, give something back that's big.

For everyone to whom much is given, from him much will be required; and to whom much has been committed, of him they will ask the more. *Luke 12:48*

262 ✦ Have a little money in the bank to handle unforeseen problems.

On the first day of the week let each one of you lay something aside, storing up as he may prosper, that there be no collections when I come. *1 Corinthians 16:2*

263 ✦ Make it a habit to do nice things for people who'll never find it out.

But when you do a charitable deed, do not let your left hand know what your right hand is doing. *Matthew 6:3*

264 ◆ Be happy with what you have while working for what you want.

I have learned in whatever state I am, to be content.
Philippians 4:11

265 ◆ When you're a guest and you're wondering if it's time to leave, it is.

Seldom set foot in your neighbor's house, lest he become weary of you and hate you. *Proverbs 25:17*

266 ◆ Learn to be comfortable with problems; that's where personal growth and opportunities lie.

My brethren, count it all joy when you fall into various trials, knowing that the testing of your faith produces patience. But let patience have its perfect work, that you may be perfect and complete, lacking nothing. *James 1:2–4*

267 · Be modest. A lot was accomplished before you were born.

Before his downfall a man's heart is proud, but humility comes before honor.   *Proverbs 18:12*

268 · Never buy a sofa too short or too fancy to sleep on.

For the bed is too short to stretch out on, and the covering so narrow that one cannot wrap himself in it. *Isaiah 28:20*

269 ✦ Put your faith to work.

As the body without the spirit is dead, so faith without deeds is dead. *James 2:26*

270 ✦ Hold your tongue when you're angry. You'll almost always be glad you did.

Even a fool is counted wise when he holds his peace; when he shuts his lips, he is considered perceptive. *Proverbs 17:28*

271 · **Remember that wealth is not having all the money you want, but having all the money you need.**

I know what it is to be in need, and I know what it is to have plenty. I have learned the secret of being content in any and every situation, whether well fed or hungry, whether living in plenty or in want.

Philippians 4:12

272 ✦ Don't argue with your mother.

The eye that mocks his father, and scorns obedience to his mother, the ravens of the valley will pick it out, and the young eagles will eat it. *Proverbs 30:17*

273 ✦ Become the world's most thoughtful friend.

A man who has friends must himself be friendly, but there is a friend who sticks closer than a brother.
Proverbs 18:24

274 ✦ Never sharpen a boomerang.

Whoever digs a pit will fall into it, and he who rolls a stone will have it roll back on him. *Proverbs 26:27*

275 ✦ Never let the odds keep you from pursuing what you know in your heart you were meant to do.

As a prisoner for the Lord, then, I urge you to live a life worthy of the calling you have received.
Ephesians 4:1

276 ◆ Share your knowledge and experience.

Likewise, teach the older women to be reverent in the way they live, not to be slanderers or addicted to much wine, but to teach what is good. Then they can train the younger women to love their husbands and children, to be self-controlled and pure, to be busy at home, to be kind, and to be subject to their husbands, so that no one will malign the word of God. *Titus 2:3–5*

277 ✦ Make your life your sermon.

You are our epistle written in our hearts, known and read by all men; clearly you are an epistle of Christ, ministered by us, written not with ink but by the Spirit of the living God, not on tablets of stone but on tablets of flesh, that is, of the heart. *2 Corinthians 3:2–3*

278 ✦ Savor every day.

This is the day the Lord has made; we will rejoice and be glad in it. *Psalm 118:24*

Books by H. Jackson Brown, Jr.

A Father's Book of Wisdom
P.S. I Love You
Life's Little Instruction Book™
    (volumes I, II, and III)
Live and Learn and Pass It On
    (volumes I, II, and III)
Wit and Wisdom from the Peanut Butter Gang
The Little Book of Christmas Joys
    (with Rosemary C. Brown and Kathy Peel)
A Hero in Every Heart
    (with Robyn Spizman)
Life's Little Treasure Books
    On Marriage and Family, On Wisdom,
    On Joy, On Success, On Love,
    On Parenting, Of Christmas Memories,
    Of Christmas Traditions, On Hope,
    On Friendship, On Fathers, On Mothers,
    On Things That Really Matter,
    On Simple Pleasures
Kids' Little Treasure Books
    On Happy Families
    On What We've Learned . . . So Far
Life's Little Instructions from the Bible
    (with Rosemary C. Brown)
Life's Little Instruction Book™ *from Mothers
to Daughters* (with Kim Shea)
Life's Little Instruction Book™ *for Incurable
Romantics* (with Robyn Spizman)

Books by Rosemary C. Brown

Rosemary Brown's Big Kitchen Instruction Book
The Little Book of Christmas Joys
    (with H. Jackson Brown, Jr., and Kathy Peel)

*Life's Little Treasure Book of Christmas
Traditions*
    (with H. Jackson Brown, Jr., and Kathy Peel)